MW00511280

WAVERLEY®
SCOTLAND

Tartan Cloth
Commonplace Notebook

If found, please contact:

____

____

____